The Codes Of Self Innovation

Five Timeless Codes of Creation to Design,
Build, and Have a Fulfilling Life

Casey E Williams
The Innovation Draftsman

First edition
Print ISBN: 978-1-0880-3846-8
EPUB ISBN: 978-1-0880-3852-9

Dedication Page

This book is dedicated to the youth of today living in a world that is deceiving and lying to you. Following the world will destroy you. Following Christ will save you.

I would also like to thank my wonderful wife Alysa for her support, help, and encouragement. Also thank you to my son Jackson for being a good sport and sleeping peacefully while we finished the final draft.

As well the contributions of Sarah Palmer and Alan Connor were priceless. And finally thanks to my friend Cameron Milligan who constantly pushed me to get 'er done.

Table of Contents

Developing The Codes

Howdy! My name is Casey (if you didn't read the cover) and I am a Texan Okie that has long felt led to be a motivational speaker ever since I witnessed Les Brown speak at the 2014 Texas FFA State Convention. Thankfully, I have waited because I gained life experience (turns out teenagers don't know as much as they think and at 24 I still have much to learn) and this book is more built on what I have learned and innovated not so much what I have invented.

How I came to develop these codes could have a short or long answer. The short answer is that I recognized these codes as a foundation of a joyful and great life. I used "codes" because, as a speaker/innovator daylighting as a cabinetry draftsman, codes are the rules one must follow by necessity; otherwise, that which you have designed will fail.

I used the term self-innovation because to innovate is to take new methods, procedures, principles, etc., and apply them to something that already exists. You are reading this book, you exist. So obviously self-innovation would be learning to innovate yourself. We don't want to re-innovate you because that would start us from scratch. You were blessed with your life (the goods and the bad); let us not throw that away but rather build off it.

Before you set off into the ensuing chapters I would like to give you a framework for the codes. These codes are not just random rules to memorize; instead they are categories to adhere to. As I said, I am a cabinetry draftsman which means there are categorical construction codes I must adhere to when designing. An example is that I must follow strict plumbing codes that dictate the spacing of plumbing features (sink, tubs, toilets, etc.) from each other and walls. One can find these codes inside the current IRC manual (International Residential Code) under the Plumbing category. There you would find diagrams, definitions, and applications to meet that category's requirements. Likewise, I jump straight into each chapter giving you definitions, concepts, examples, and applications to help you meet the requirements of each Code of Self Innovation in your own life.

It is my hope that any reader might be able to use this book and these codes to design a life that is filled with Truth, Self-Discipline, Morality, Contentment, and Fulfillment. Doing so will produce a strength, purpose, and joy that will redefine your approach to life. So... are you ready to Have A Great Life?

Chapter 1

Story Time!

Could you believe that introduction was the short answer?! Well, that is because the long answer takes a winding backroad of the past to demonstrate how I learned the codes. I don't want to make this chapter my autobiography but the following is important because you could refer to me as a jack of all trades master of none; but that is not entirely true. In fact, I am actually a master of one thing–failure.

Family Matters

The entrepreneur spirit and the jimmy-rig-it spirit runs strong in my family. Everybody knows somebody that is handy and for me, those handy people were my PawPaw and Dad. I spent many hours, growing up, following them around and slowly merged their influences into my own life, ambitions, and ideas. PawPaw used to make all types of contraptions; sometimes to solve a problem and sometimes just for fun (a specialty he had was making 2,3, or even 4 person bicycles). He loved grabbing and storing bits of "junk" either to repair it or reuse it for another project. Along with fixing things, PawPaw also owned the first self-serve gas station in our town (at a time when that was unheard of for a small town), a laundromat, and a car wash. Over time he acquired the family land, and some, to build a small cattle operation that runs to this day. Further, he did all of this while working for the railroad, which he retired from after retiring from the military (Granny and the kids played no small part in the process).

Pawpaw is my mother's father, yet my dad shares similar characteristics learned from Papa (his father) and PawPaw. My dad is also a great handyman as well as a businessman. You tend to (try and) fix anything and everything out in the country; always willing to help, I was the assistant to many repairs growing up. Whether it is a vehicle, tractor, UTV, or washing machine Dad has had to try his hand at fixing it all and then some. Beyond the honey-do list and farm work, he's also a business major turned teacher with numerous business ideas over time. He distinctly recalls having theorized how newspapers someday will no longer need to be physical (before the internet) and also a method for wireless calling (before Bluetooth). Did he create the technology? No. But he actively practiced forward-thinking on recognizing and theorizing how to resolve tomorrow's problems. While he might not have become wealthy from the ideas, innovation is a great trait not everyone actively pursues or practices. At one time, he did have a goal to be a millionaire before he was 30 but that changed when a wealthy local gave him some advice. When looking at my dad with his wife and 4 boys the man said "you're the wealthiest man in town with that family". That perspective caused my dad to be content with whatever was best for his family instead of pursuing the vanity of money to symbolize they had "made it". Yep, forget the corporate world, a teacher's salary was good enough for the ability to live on/manage PawPaw's land, have the same schedule and vacation as us kids, and carry on the tradition of DIY repairs till you can't any more.

I grew up with every member of my family having hair-brained ideas for businesses, products, and much more. Mix that in with following after the thinker/tinkerer spirits of two patriarchs and you have a recipe for somebody that is, frankly, always up to no good. I don't have stories of tearing apart toys to see how they worked or something extreme like that. I just had a constant desire to use what was accessible and innovate it into something new. Unfortunately, ideas are proven through failure and life likes to teach the best lessons when you have fallen on your face. I have certainly had my hiccups but I wouldn't trade the ups and downs because they have taught me plenty of lessons. I have some key failures that I would like to share but each failure has molded a greater ability for success.

The Drummer Boy Evolution

Of my notable failures, the first started in high school when I invented a new type of drum pedal. I had always loved drumming but being a heathen too unfocused to learn the discipline, I devised a way to play without as much practice. If you are like me, you can bounce your leg up and down rapidly, easily tapping your heel; however, drummers tap their toe to play the kick drum which is exhausting to the untrained (like me). So I wanted to make a reverse drum pedal that played the bass drum at the tap of your heel instead of your toe. With a donated drum pedal and help from my dad and his shop, I was able to create a working prototype! I really thought it was a revolutionary idea and I was all that and a bag of chips. These babies were going to sell like hotcakes and I'd be rich! However, my invention was short-lived because I soon discovered someone had already filed a patent for a similar design; which for an inventor is no bueno. Unfortunately, you can't sell a product that matches another's design while their patent is active so I pocketed the experience gained and shelved the prototype.

If I remember correctly, the drum pedal project ran from the spring semester of my freshman year to the beginning of the following school year. While it was disappointing to stop the project, I didn't sit idle for long because the next creation came in my junior year.

The Videographer's Dream

I've always been into action sports which inspired me to create a product that would help filming skate and BMX videos. I went to the drawing board and came up with a good design, aided by the Mechanical Drafting class I was taking at my high school. During the process, I discovered once again I was late to the party but this time my invention-turned-innovation was a different approach to a similar design, so I was clear to pursue it. This project, The Stingray action camera stabilizer, lasted from junior year into freshman year of college because I really believed in its potential. Over time, I perfected my design, talked with a small business advisor, received quotes for production, filed for patent pending status, and was even considered for a knock-off Shark Tank TV show! (Though nothing became of the show). I can't begin to tell you all the hats I had to wear to work on this project from mechanical drafting to graphic design to marketing. When you create something you either must do it all, find someone that can, or give up; in the famous (infamous?) words of Shia LaBeouf "Just Do It!". When I discovered the manufacturing quotes were far out of my price range I wasn't deterred. I worked with my youth pastor to 3-D print my latest prototype so I could start selling them – but alas the unassembled parts are in my closet to this day.

What happened? I had every reason to find even marginal success. Well, throughout those three years I was at the peak of my get-rich-quick mindset which meant I often spent only 30% of my energy on The Stingray and weighed myself down with other ideas. In college, a friend expressed a comment that I still think about regularly because of how well it describes me. When trying to rebrand my YouTube channel he offered the name of "Whole A**ing Nothing" I want to keep this PG but this comment is important. When I watched *Parks and Rec* sometime later I truly realized what my friend 'Murray had said. The character Ron Swanson tells of a key change in his life as a child when he concluded "never half-a** two things. Whole a** one thing". 'Murray had wisely seen what I was doing and my desire to Whole-Butt Nothing rightly lead to failure time and time again. The product never worked out because I was never willing to truly give it the time and energy it needed. The easiest path to "success" and money was always more enticing and new ideas were always coming.

Falling Into Film and Horses

While in between invention #2 and #3, I dropped out of college just after freshman year because I couldn't settle on a major. Providentially, I got hooked up to work on an indie film that following summer, which gave me something promising without heading back to the grocery store. I quickly became known as "the runner" of *The Runners* movie and had a blast working with a small crew in that sweltering Texas June. Initially, I had become interested in film because I wanted to pursue screen acting and thanks to that experience (and having a local monopoly on Production Assistants for hire (films lowest rung)) I fell into the film industry as a crew member. Over my two years on and off different sets, I set (no pun intended) myself apart with a willingness to always have "open hands" (a statement that

Including my architectural drafting degree that I will discuss later, I have completed 90% of two associate's degrees and 75% completed a bachelor's of communication. All that school and debt with only a certificate to show for it, and I rightly blame myself. A quick comment, life will fly by, yes college or whatever might seem like it will never end but you've got many years left to finish what you started and do everything else. Impatience led me to squander having a bachelor's degree in two years!

you are ready to help) and work from the first minute to the last, even with occasional 16+ hour days. Any filmmaker will attest that it is a labor of love that keeps you going on never-ending projects, and that may be so, but it's also a great place for those who just love a hard day's work, traveling, and solving unique situations.

One thing important that happened in the middle of my film career was falling in love with racehorses. Film can be a little slow in the Texas winters so I got a job I had long been curious about. You see, my lifelong friend, Cameron, is the son of Mr. Eddie who had a two-year-old racehorse training operation in my hometown. Having become interested in horse racing via my friend and being a rural AG kid I always wondered what it would be like to work for Mr. Eddie. I got my chance on the first Monday after Christmas 2016 and it was fantastic. Being up close with horses for the first time in my life was an awesome experience and that peaceful barn will always have a place in my heart.

Horse Dummies and Race Cars

Shortly after starting my job of mucking out horse stalls, Mr. Eddie put a bug in my ear to make a horse training dummy. So I did. The first iteration was very rough but it got us moving in the right direction and even though I only worked there for three months my dummy project kept going. For two years, components, parts, supplies, and a dummy (in various phases) rode in the back of my SUV. In the end, I had worked with three separate trainers to perfect the dummy into a very good, usable product. By this time

I was eager to start selling the dummies to prospective operations. I knew it wouldn't sell millions but I believed in the mission and would have been thrilled just to sell 100 a year. Sadly however my dreams of grandeur died simply because I wasn't willing to step into the role of salesman. I've always been happy to put on any cap but when it comes to selling I always used the excuse of needing someone else to do it. I have three business majors in my immediate family, I'm not the business and sales guy - I'm just the idea guy. That broken thinking kept me from ever leveraging my abilities to accomplish more.

Successful businesses are indeed built on leaders that recognize their strengths and weaknesses and hire others more qualified. Consider how an excellent marketer built the world's most known computer brand. Steve Jobs couldn't

Note on businesses, the consumer will verify the viability of a product in the end; It is the business' obligation to deliver the best product possible.

build a computer but Steve Wozniak could and Jobs' attitude drove the ship to success. Saying I wasn't a salesman was just an excuse to quit. Sure others have skills I don't but that is no reason to give up. Instead, adversity teaches one to cultivate their abilities and hire/promote those strong where they are weak for the fullest pursuit of a goal.

After leaving the horses, I got a job doing grounds maintenance at *Rally Ready Driving School* near Austin, TX. Now this job was the ultimate dream come true. I had a job I liked, a sport I loved, and the region I admired. I spent my days mowing, raking the track, fixing mowers, getting things stuck, and watching cars skid through gravel. I even was able to score a couple of 10-minute crash courses consisting of a half day's training. My dreams of being a racecar driver had found their beginning! Yet even though everything screamed my name, I found myself discontent for no particular reason and I was ready to leave after only a month.

In hindsight, my willingness to jump around ruined my ability to learn and grow in a new job. I've Jones'd over what could've been had I been reliable and just enjoyed the ride working for Mr. Eddie or at Rally Ready. On the one hand, I could be traveling around the world racing cars; and on the other, I could be the prodigy of a successful horse trainer. This reality fights to keep me humbled and more patient to this day.

I also made a poor choice to sort of walk away suddenly instead of being upfront and giving advance notice (thankfully we are good now).

Slightly More Edjumacated

Well no more cars meant back to film I went... that is until the movie *Dunkirk* gave me the idea to be a fighter pilot. So I went back to school, since having a degree helps with those things (Casey logic is -well ... unique). You can imagine the roller coaster my friends and family went on if this retelling is only the half of it.

Ever since my parents designed their house I wanted to be an architect (something my crazy ideas made me forget) so when I went back to school it was for architecture. Initially, I had hoped to use Austin Community College as a springboard into Architecture school but it actually sent me down a better path to be a draftsman instead. I stuck with it for once and learned how to do a job and have a career. The only problem was that I discovered horses have a way of getting under your skin. I love drafting but as semesters went on my desire to return to the racehorses only grew more and more. So, I settled with a certificate (2 classes away from an Associates…) and Mr. Eddie got me a new job working on the racetrack for one of America's top trainers!

This time I made a promise to myself that I was going to stick with it for at least a year and that's what I did. I moved my tiny RV to Louisiana and started walking horses for the assistant trainer, Jay. I've always been introverted but over time I have forced myself to talk and that started in Louisiana. I was quiet to be sure but I asked questions, was personable, learned from many, and received increased responsibility and side jobs for my willingness to get my hands dirty.

School-shmool, Barn Living Is The Life For Me

Horse racing stables travel in circuits that repeat each year, dictated by the annual schedule of each track you plan to race at (Jay has been on the same circuit for over a decade). Louisiana changed to Dallas and then eventually Oklahoma City. While in Dallas, I was promoted to a groom (think equine caretaker) and began learning how to care for a horse while working twice a day, no matter the cold or heat, seven days a week (holidays included). Eventually, it almost literally becomes like brushing your teeth; before I reached that time, my coworkers joked how I was an old man because I hobbled around for most of my first 4 months grooming. Over time and much stretching, I eventually accustomed my body to the task until Jay's plan was accomplished to make me a lean mean grooming machine. Approaching the 9 month mark I was content to continue this path until I could take out a trainer's license and start my own stable.

Now We're Up To Now

So what's the haps now? Well for starters, I learned that everyone needs an occasional vacation. But more importantly, in Oklahoma City, I met the woman of my dreams and I was smart enough to know that sticking around was the better choice by far. So I did my year's labor and used my drafting knowledge to get a job locally designing cabinets.

I got the job and the girl, why bother writing a book? Well because my biggest passion in life (even more than architecture) has been to be a motivational speaker. I love my life but I was tired of saying "one day" or never making it happen. Now that I knew my weaknesses and strengths, had a gal in my corner, and was now an expert at failure, it was time to make this passion a reality. Ultimately the delay has been for the best because my message has progressed over time. For many years I have been a Christian but over the most recent years I have attempted to truly grow in my faith (by the Work of the Spirit) and in that time my ideas have shifted from being a mindless fluff-motivator to a better desire to provide motivation that is more concrete. Through various means, I have seen how our post-Christian world is in desperate need of morality, structure, truth, hope, and a reason for purpose and joy. The arguments I will make in the following chapters come from personal experience, the wisdom of others, and most importantly from the world's most valuable and best-selling book, the Holy Bible. My hope is to demonstrate these codes are just highlights of standard rules seen throughout history and that they are foundational to creation.

Above all, may this book lead to you having a great life, knowing and believing the Gospel of Christ, and fulfilling your ultimate calling. As the Westminster Shorter Catechism expounds:

"What is the chief end of man?"

"Man's chief end is to glorify God and enjoy him forever"

Chapter 2

Truth

Let's start the chapter titled truth with a dose of it.

Every ethnicity has at one time or another either been enslaved or enslaved others. Slavery is an industry thousands of years old and one that continues to exist today even though its popularity has rightfully waned. So if that is a fact then it means saying America or England (via America) invented slavery is false/a lie. But if America didn't found slavery why do so many people argue otherwise? Well for starters they don't practice truth or seek it out; juicy gossip, slander, and hearsay are more their interest. But the West gets singled out because rather than perpetuating slavery they repented of it and abolished it!

Numerous Northern states sought to abolish slavery as far back as the founding of Jamestown and the Mayflower Compact. Britain became the first nation to abolish slavery and used their global power to affect the change. America followed suit later but sadly, while other nations peacefully abolished slavery, hundreds of thousands of Americans had to die in the

Civil War before slavery was officially axed. The West didn't invent slavery but they recognized it as the evil it was and for the first time in history set a new, anti-slavery norm and standard. That is true.

Operation Downfall was a proposed plan to invade Japan during World War II. Though Germany had surrendered, Japan showed no signs of giving up even though they were losing the war in the Pacific. Had Operation Downfall taken place it is likely to have resulted in the deaths of millions of Allied troops and many more millions of Japanese troops and civilian conscripts (taught to be suicide bombers, fighters, etc.) with estimations as high as 15 million dead before Japan maybe surrendered. Instead of pursuing many more years of war and death the choice was made to drop the atomic bombs on Japan, resulting in the deaths of 300-500 thousand.

Once Japan had surrendered, General MacArthur was sent to reform Japan and you may find it interesting to know that MacArthur not only sought to affect Japan in government and society but also in religion. MacArthur requested thousands of Christian missionaries to come minister to Japan and he had bibles heavily distributed. Within 7 years Japan was such a radically different nation that they were permitted reentry into the United Nations. That is also true.

The reason why I bring these two stories up is because it bucks the narrative commonly pushed in leftist academia and media today. But also, both of these stories have a common theme outside of being true, that is they were backed by truth. Christianity and the Bible were foundationally involved in the creation of America and the potent effect of God's word has positively changed many nations, Japan included. Andrew Stebbins says *"Any serious and unbiased observer of social development will acknowledge that 'religion has played a leading role in directing the course of history.'"*[1] If we desire to continue to promote progress and goodness in our own lives, communities and nations we must follow suit and believe in and be supported by truth.

What Is Truth Anyways?

Truth is subjective. I have my truth, you have your truth. We can agree or disagree. My truth can say your truth is false and vice versa but that's ok. We can just gather around the campfire and all sing Kumbaya.

You've probably heard people talk like that or you yourself talk like that. The problem is that the above paragraph is a load of bullcrap. You have your opinions and I have mine and that's ok; but, truth is universal—black and white. For example, it is true, ie fact, that you can't breathe in outer space (no aids permitted). If I say true and you say false that doesn't mean you magically develop the ability to breathe in the vacuum of outer space. It is either true or it is false. You can voice opinions, hypotheses, studies, etc. that speak on the parameters of the hypothetical situation, what constitutes "breathing", etc. but at the end of the day we will all die in outer space without some type of aid.

---

[1] Stebbins, Andrew. "How Christianity Shaped Western Civilization." Reasons to Believe, 22 Apr. 2021, https://reasons.org/explore/blogs/reflections/how-christianity-shaped-western-civilization.

What you believe to be true and how firmly you believe said truth radically shapes how you live your life. If you firmly believed that the old saying "step on a crack, break your momma's back" was true (and you loved your mother) you would obsess about cracks. What constitutes a "back-breaking" crack? Do cracks in all materials/elements count (concrete, dirt, tile, etc.)? If you theoretically could walk upside down, would cracks in a ceiling count? The list goes on and on of how you would center your life on avoiding cracks so as to not break your dear mother's back. But there is a more important question to ask first– is it true?

The fact of the crack is that it can't magically break backs? (keyword is "magically", obviously there are situations where this is plausible and possible). At the end of the day, the health of your mother's back is not hinged on your ability to avoid cracks even if you believed it with all your heart.

So what is truly true and how can we know it? I'm glad (I assume) you asked. There are some things in this life that we can know are true no matter our location, identity, opinions, etc. They are true to existence itself and they are true in spite of us. I would like to share these truths with you. I didn't develop these truths on a warm summer's morning drinking butter-coffee on a mountainside (though that sounds nice); I simply recog-

The verse in question was Romans 5:12 which discusses how Adam was humanity's representative and Christ is the representative of the Church and humanity 2.0. Steve Lawson's Men's Bible Study has a couple lessons on this for a better explanation then I can give.

nized/learned them and am sharing them with you.

Building a foundation of truth is…well foundational to have a fulfilling life. Where we fall on defin-
ing truth and applying said definition will result in us
arriving at radically different conclusions. I was listen-
ing to a Bible study the other day and the Pastor was
emphasizing how one's interpretation of a specific
verse will completely predict/dictate their interpretation of the rest of the Bible. That sounds pretty important to get right then, huh? As I have just recently
illustrated, what you believe is very important. I have
shared the following truths to wet your appetite and
begin shoring up your foundations.

Complex problems can be simple when you break them down into concepts you understand (or Complex tasks can be completed by incremental progress)

Let's start off easy. "*Complex problems can be simple when you break them down into concepts you understand*". This is seen most clearly by considering the six
simple machines: the lever, pulley, wheel and axle, inclined plane, wedge, and screw. The simple machines
employ rudimentary methods of physics and science
to operate but the principles within them greatly help
us understand complex machines.

Consider having to design a car with no auto-
motive knowledge–seems daunting right? Well let's
break it down! For starters it rolls because of the
Wheel and Axle, so that's easy! Also, the engine drives
the wheels because it is attached by rotating shafts
which are essentially examples of the Wheel and Axle
machine. Inside each piston housing (cylinder), the

combustion engine repeatedly compresses an air-fuel mixture till it explodes (due to physics and chemistry) and that micro-controlled explosion pushes the piston down. This piston is connected to another piston mirrored on the other side of the engine; when one moves down the other moves up which causes another explosion-by-compression which causes the cycle to repeat. This constant push and pull of the pistons are most directly akin to the Pulley. But you also see evidence of the wedge because of the compression, and also examples of levers via weights that keep the pistons balanced and in rhythm. So in a rather rough speedy approach we can see the presence of various simple machines working together to make the complex machine of an automobile. I could go on but I hope you can see that something complex can be understood when broken down into simple terms. For a final, simpler analogy let's do some quick math.

We all know $2 + 2 = 4$ but also $2 \times 2 = 4$. This is because multiplication is just condensed addition. 2 items plus 2 more items equals 4 total items, which represents addition. But also 2 groups consisting of 2 items each also equals 4 total items. If we use larger numbers, we know that there are 12 inches in a foot. If you measure a wall that is 5 feet long that means you have 5 groups, each consisting of 12 inches. If you added up 12+12+12+12+12 you get... 12 then 24 then 36 then 48 then 60 total inches! Multiplication is just the shortcut that says 5 groups of 12 is also 60!

When life throws you a difficult problem just break it down to things that you understand and it will be easier to grasp. Back in the ancient yesteryear of high school, my youth pastor Justin would connect his computer to the projector to show us videos of various learning sorts. (Tim Hawkins can be educational!) During this process, his inspirational desktop wallpaper was often plastered across the wall while the different programs booted it up; it was through this that I began to internalize the inspirational quote. With a picture of a giant elephant it read "How do you eat an elephant? One bite at a time." If you're like me you initially need an explanation but I hope it becomes in grained in you as well. How do you eat an elephant? Well one bite at a time of course!

Elephants are huge don't you know! I've seen some food eating contests but I don't think Kobayashi or Joey Chestnut could eat an elephant in one sitting let alone one bite! Big challenges, problems, goals, etc. take an incremental progress to complete. A similar idea is described in the book Atomic Habits where you strive to get 1% better at "x" and over many days and months and years you'll look back to see the progress you didn't realize you made! (The 10,000 hour rule is also the same idea).

> *I still have yet to read Atomic Habits by James Clear but I've heard some successful people recommend it.*

You are a unique, irreplaceable human being

Another truth is *"You are a unique, irreplaceable human being"*. Only you have existed in your exact situation, with your exact parents, location, friends, education, etc. You are uniquely one of a kind. Be comforted, that you are not alone even though you are unique. We all have our own uniqueness but other people have gone through similar or relatable experiences, and they can help us through ours. Humans are community creatures and having someone in the trenches with you is a great aid for your positive progress in any area.

Maybe you're struggling in school, or have a rough family life (call the police if your or another's life is in danger), maybe relationships are hard, etc. take comfort in knowing that there are people that have experienced life that can help you. You need others' and they need you. Reach out to others and ask for help; the first person you come across might not have the answers but don't give up. Many times, even when you ask the wrong person they have recommendations on finding the right people to talk to.

I always think of the TV show *The West Wing* when it comes to this topic because of a story shared when Leo tries to help Josh in his time of need, saying this:

This guy's walking down a street, when he falls in a hole. The walls are so steep. He can't get out.

A doctor passes by, and the guy shouts up "Hey you! Can you help me out?" The doctor writes him a prescription, throws it down the hole and moves on.

Then a priest comes along and the guy shouts up "Father, I'm down in this hole, can you help me out?" The priest writes out a prayer, throws it down in the hole and moves on.

Then a friend walks by. "Hey Joe, it's me, can you help me out?" And the friend jumps in the hole! Our guy says "Are you stupid? Now we're both down here!" and the friend says, "Yeah, but I've been down here before, and I know the way out." [West Wing: Season Two, Episodes 10." Warner, 2000.]

You were created in the image of God and are therefore a wonderfully unique individual that can only affect the world in your particular way. Don't waste your life and influence but rather use your time here for the betterment of those around you. To steal from the wise sage Zig Ziglar *"You can have everything in life you want if you will just help enough other people get what they want."* And through it all, associate yourself with people that are a positive influence and that will rebuke you so as to make you better, even when it's hard to hear.

BONUS: Other Zig Ziglar Quotes I found trying to find the "Help Others" Quote

If you don't plan your time, someone else will help you waste it.

You never know when a moment and a few sincere words can have an impact on a life.

There will always be people in your life who treat you wrong. Be sure to thank them for making you strong.

You were created for a purpose

Life is valuable and so are you because… (wait for it…..) *"You were created for a purpose"*! This is the next truth and we are slowly digging a little deeper with each truth. Some of you might have had alarms going when I used that little word "created" but that's a-ok because it is an important word. Yes, you were created and with your creation, you were given a purpose.

Subtitles kind of ruin the surprise huh? I've always been bad about glancing ahead personally so it's likely a moot point.

Before I can truly encourage you on what your purpose is, I must answer the angry people ready to burn this book. You see, people get all up in arms by the idea that the universe was created because they are "smart" and they have "science" to back them up. First, let's bring in our first truth and break this down simply. You have likely seen/owned a smartphone. If I told you that that small device, with more computation ability than Apollo 13, came out of a wormhole in the Bermuda Triangle you'd think I was crazy. Why? Well, we all know that our phone is a product of incredible engineers, computer scientists, marketers, technicians, workers, machines, etc. and to say that it came out of a wormhole is to slander their hard work. As complicated as the most advanced machine in the universe is /could be, the universe itself is infinitely more complex.

Consider how the entire universe works seamlessly with one another. The Earth is at the perfect distance from the Sun to neither burn up nor freeze. The Earth "conveniently" has plants that consume Carbon Dioxide and make Oxygen as a byproduct; animals "conveniently" need this byproduct and in turn, create Carbon Dioxide to continue the cycle. Even with "evidence" to support evolution, no scientist has found a species in the middle of transitioning to another species. Conveniently we just "happen" to be living at the perfect amount of billions of years required to have consistent species.

Everyone likes to say Plato and many others were incredibly wise yet they have abandoned their belief in Biological Essentialism. Biological Essentialism states that biology exists within certain types and kinds, and moving categories is impossible. We can see that dogs, wolves, and coyotes have a common ancestry and are the same type but to say that a dog can become a fish is clearly ludicrous– they are two separate and distinct kinds. It wasn't until Darwin witnessed finches having some differences from other finches that he began to fabricate the notion of evolution.

We have long understood animals change simply by adaptation, or slight changes within their kind. Consider all the breeds of domestic dogs. Their ancestry is that of the wolf but how did a wolf become a corgi, dachshund, or poodle? Simple. These domestic breeds were created via selective breeding by humans to draw out certain traits over time. Likewise, Darwin's finches adapted to acting and looking different from other finches because their environment was different. Darwin proved adaptation exists but he came nowhere near evolution– if he had, he would have found franken-finches in the midst of changing kinds.

The only "evidence" to support evolution is the evidence found by those causing

Most scientists practice storytelling not science. Just read some of their reports on what took place millions of years ago! They regularly formulate hypothesis (as science must) but then treat their own theories as hard fact. Often it is just an elaborate tale.

the evidence to be anything worth looking at. Reading their research papers requires following the "scientist" through hoops that have no rational connection other than their ability to say "because I said so". If you would like to learn more on Biological Essentialism, a friend of mine, Jay Hall wrote a book on the matter heavily relying on smart people to prove the point for him. I hope you can begin to see that evolution is just a theory as much as mermaids and that when you really think about it, the world is far too perfectly placed together to have been some cosmic accident. If it had been a cosmic accident there would be a wormhole creating smartphones in the Bermuda Triangle but there is nothing of the sort. Instead, everything works together seamlessly and consistently.

Bonus! Did you know that the Big Bang Theory was created by a catholic priest? Georges Lemaître developed this theory at a time when the universe had long been believed to be static, and after Edwin Hubble discovered evidence of the universe expanding, the later named Big Bang Theory was accepted. This is notable because the theory begs the question of what banged, how did it get there, and why? If a long long time ago there was nothing (and God didn't exist) then today there would be nothing. Nothing = Nothing....clearly. All pointing to the necessity of a creator. While it may be theory, it goes to show that science supports a creator...when the scientists aren't blinded by atheistic bias.

Truth is known through the Holy Bible

The primary source material that the Founding Fathers used to establish the unique nation of America was the best-selling and most preserved book of all time, the Holy Bible.

> *The great, vital, and conservative element in our system is the belief of our people in the pure doctrines and the divine truths of the Gospel of Jesus Christ. [United States House Judiciary Committee of Congress 1854]*

The Holy Bible was preserved for thousands of years by the Jewish people and that tradition has been continued by Christians ever since the last book of the New Testament was completed prior to 100 A.D. Just as a comparison, there have been over 5-7 Billion copies of the Bible printed, and the manuscript tradition includes over 25,000 New Testament manuscripts (for comparison Homer's *Iliad* has roughly 1800). The reason why the Bible is so important is because it is known to be the infallible, inerrant word of God.

As the Westminster Shorter Catechism states "The Word of God, which is contained in the scriptures of the Old and New Testaments, is the only rule to direct us how we may glorify and enjoy Him [God]." This is important because if it is true it should shape our approach to life. This statement claims A) that there is a God, B) He expects something from us (i.e. gives us a purpose), and C) the Bible is the means to learn this.

Can we trust the Bible? The Bible is the only sure means to find truth because no other book so sufficiently and effectively answers how and why we are here within itself, with its prestige, and without contradiction (reading the Bible as a whole and not removing pieces from their context). It is also the only book that offers a complete, unique, and true salvation. Other religions tell you how you should do x,y, and z to prove your goodness so that you may have some type of favorable life after you die.

Even Atheism is a religion that tells you this life is all you get so, while you could live it up, you should be a good person while you are here (stealing often from a Christian worldview to have morals in a system that can't support or create them).

Can I prove any of this? Sure, the first evidence is that we have a conscience and the law of God is written on our hearts.

[Rom 2:14-15 NASB95] 14 For when Gentiles who do not have the Law do instinctively the things of the Law, these, not having the Law, are a law to themselves, 15 in that they show the work of the Law written in their hearts, their conscience bearing witness and their thoughts alternately accusing or else defending them

We all know that lying, adultery, theft, and murder are all wrong things to do. Now being wicked, we typically justify lying when it's a little white lie, or we think that adultery is fine if it is mutual or never discovered. There are even times when we justify stealing things because it's small, that is the owner won't notice or we think we deserve it. Further, some people will say that murder can be justifiable or excusable because the victim was a bad person (self-defense isn't murder) or that the killer is good deep down. Ultimately we all like to excuse ourselves or loved ones from wrongdoing but we condemn anyone that wrongs us in any way. The fact of the matter is, we almost universally know that those four crimes, and others, are wrong (how we are raised does influence our lenses towards them).

The Bible does not excuse our lax opinions, however; all liars will have their place in the lake of fire (Rev 21:8) and thieves will not inherit the Kingdom of God (1 Cor 6:10). Jesus tells us that anyone who has lusted after another has committed adultery in their heart (Matt 5:21-22), or if anyone has hated another they have committed murder in their heart (Matt 5:27-28).

We also learn from the Bible that all of creation tells of God and we are therefore fools to deny His existence in light of His handiwork.

[Psa 19:1 NASB95] 1 ...The heavens are telling of the glory of God; And their expanse is declaring the work of His hands.

[Rom 1:18-22 NASB95] 18 For the wrath of God is revealed from heaven against all ungodliness and unrighteousness of men who suppress the truth in unrighteousness, 19 because that which is known about God is evident within them; for God made it evident to them. 20 For since the creation of the world His invisible attributes, His eternal power and divine nature, have been clearly seen, being understood through what has been made, so that they are without excuse. 21 For even though they knew God, they did not honor Him as God

or give thanks, but they became futile in their speculations, and their foolish heart was darkened. 22 Professing to be wise, they became fools,

If you read Romans 1-3 you will find a very complete condemnation of every one of us for we have all sinned and fallen short of the glory of God (Romans 3:23). In a very direct way, we see that in Paul's first letter to the Corinthians.

[1Co 6:9-11 NASB95] 9 Or do you not know that the un-righteous will not inherit the kingdom of God? Do not be deceived; neither fornicators, nor idolaters, nor adulterers, nor effeminate, nor homosexuals, 10 nor thieves, nor [the] covetous, nor drunkards, nor revilers, nor swindlers, will inherit the kingdom of God. 11 Such were some of you; but you were washed, but you were sanctified, but you were justified in the name of the Lord Jesus Christ and in the Spirit of our God.

The bad news is we all are guilty in one or more of those categories and therefore we will never make it to heaven BUT we do have hope for escape. In verse 11 Paul references that his audience was guilty of these sins but "such were some of you" implies that they have found freedom, namely freedom in "the Lord Jesus Christ and in the Spirit of our God." This is where we see the final support of the Bible that I am going to mention at this time because this freedom is something that no other religion offers. The religions of man suggest you need to prove yourself to make it into heaven but Paul mentions that Jesus justified them not their works.

The Good News You and I Desperately Need

I promise I will keep this as short as possible but let me tie up the loose ends I have created. I have attempted to show you that truth exists, that God is the source of truth, and that the Bible teaches us God's truth. The final thing I would like to express is that Jesus is our only hope for heavenly bliss.

[Jhn 14:6 NASB95] 6 Jesus said to him, "I am the way, and the truth, and the life; no one comes to the Father but through Me.

In the words of C.S. Lewis "Jesus was either a liar, lunatic, or Lord." (Thomas Aquinas said it long before Lewis but it typically gets accredited to Lewis since he is a contemporary writer) Either John 14:6 is true or it is not. If it is false, then Jesus either intentionally lied or He believed it and was therefore just a loony; but, if He was telling the truth then we are required to recognize Him as Lord. If Jesus was telling the truth then we have no hope of ever entering heaven except through Him and if we don't go to heaven when we die that means we must instead go to hell for our disobedience.

The Gospel (Good News) of Jesus Christ is this. That we have sinned against God and because God is just He must punish us for our lawlessness. But God being rich in mercy and love for us sent His son into the world to live the life that we could not live (sinless and perfect), so that He could suffer the death that we deserved for our sins on the cross, paying the blood debt that we could never afford. In doing so our sins were accredited to Him and His righteousness was accredited to us so that God's justice could be fulfilled. With God having accepted the atoning work of Christ on the cross, Christ rose from the dead in bodily form proclaiming His victory over death and sin. Only in the Bible and Christianity will you find a complete salvation that does not rest on our merits but rather on the merits of one who is actually perfect and right-eous.

Have you ever noticed how all the world's reli-gions/systems are conflicting yet at the end of the day they are pretty cool with each other? For example, the LGBT community tears apart the Bible and its con-demnation against their identifying sin yet they don't say much on how some Mus-lims believe sodomy (homo-sexuality) is worthy of death. Nor do very many feminists attack Muslim beliefs on their difference between men and women, but the Bible saying that men and women have separate yet complementary roles is terrible. Also, have you noticed that Christmas and Easter (the two biggest Chris-tian holidays) have become so heavily commercialized that the holiday now revolves around Santa Claus and an egg-laying bunny, instead of about Jesus?

> To be a sodomite is to practice sexual per-version. This is a per-version of what is the right function of a man and a woman (more in a later chap-ter). The term sodo-mite refers to the peo-ple of Sodom who were destroyed by God's wrath for their sin.

Most comical to me is how atheists believe there is not a god and then are often consumed with the need to disprove the Bible to validate their unbelief. If God doesn't exist then why do they spend so much time and energy trying to prove to you their conclusion? I'd say because the recruitment of other atheists is giving them a false sense of security that God doesn't exist. This is seen so clearly by the presentation of the Law of God, such as the ten Commandments, or the Gospel. In fact, including this in the book is likely guaranteeing negative reviews and no further progress for some readers unwilling to confront this truth.

> [1 Co 1:23 NASB95] but we preach Christ crucified, to Jews a stumbling block and to Gentiles foolishness

I could have placed this section at the back of the book but the remaining Codes of Self-Innovation are useless by themselves in giving you a better life. This is because not believing the Gospel is to ruin your present and eternal life by never receiving the true source of security, purpose, and joy.

The Exclusivity of Christ

C.S. Lewis also said, "Christianity, if false, is of no importance, and if true, of infinite importance, the only thing it cannot be is moderately important." The one question everyone must ask of themselves is "what am I going to believe about Jesus?" Either Jesus is The Way, The Truth, and The Life or He is not. Other religions often have a good person "merit badge" that universally lets anyone in even if you deny their god. Christianity says you must believe in Christ alone and have your faith fully placed in Him, His completed work of salvation for your sins, and His victorious bodily resurrection from the grave. If you are not willing to believe that or you believe that

Christ died for your sins yet you need to contribute something to earn your place then you are damned already. Salvation is by grace alone through faith alone in Christ alone according to the scriptures alone for the glory of God alone.

You can deny what I have said here but you will never be able to disprove it and even if you are fully convinced I am wrong you will still never cease to war with your conscience and Christ.

Hold on to these truths and study the Word of God to build upon them and be further rooted in a firm, unshakable foundation. The remaining Codes are very helpful and beneficial but also a complete waste of time without being completely surrendered to the Lordship of Christ.

Made Alive In Christ

[Eph 2:1-10 NASB95] 1 And you were dead in your trespasses and sins, 2 in which you formerly walked according to the course of this world, according to the prince of the power of the air, of the spirit that is now working in the sons of disobedience. 3 Among them we too all formerly lived in the lusts of our flesh, indulging the desires of the flesh and of the mind, and were by nature children of wrath, even as the rest. 4 But God, being rich in mercy, because of His great love with which He loved us, 5 even when we were dead in our transgressions, made us alive together with Christ (by grace you have been saved), 6 and raised us up with Him, and seated us with Him in the heavenly [places] in Christ Jesus, 7 so that in the ages to come He might show the surpassing riches of His grace in kindness toward us in Christ Jesus. 8 For by grace you have been saved through faith; and that not of yourselves, [it is] the gift of God; 9 not as a result of works, so that no one may boast. 10 For we are His workmanship, created in Christ Jesus for good works, which God prepared beforehand so that we would walk in them.

Chapter 3

Self-Discipline

Imagine a group of kids playing kickball by a cliff's edge. If they did not have a fence, you can imagine them being extra careful to chase the ball, once it neared the edge. However, if they had a tall sight-blocking fence along the cliff's edge, they would play freely even though death is only inches away.

Another example, If you have ever dealt much with children (or you may recall from your childhood) you likely have noticed how kids handle "rules". Any time kids are playing a self-governed game, the "leader" will almost always change the rules when they are likely to lose. After a few of these "executive orders", you will soon have a kid-congress in-session as young politicians argue the merits of the existing rules and proposed new rules. This anarchy comes about when there is not a third-party making and enforcing the rules. When the latter is available, the children freely play to their hearts' content.

As we have seen in these two examples children love structure and rules (though they might act and say otherwise). Even though we get older, that characteristic never changes.

Self-discipline is the second code because it is the construction worker building your house of HAGL (working from the foundation of truth). Unfortunately we humans are difficult creatures and we love to make excuses so you will need first to ask for discipline. Yes, you can't make any progress towards self-discipline on your own; you need the help of others. Just like the kids in the above examples, the best source of discipline and structure are adults that could build the fence and referee the game. Hopefully, you have/had wise parents that have not been ashamed to discipline you when growing up. (It might not be physical punishment always and abuse is obviously not permissible). Consider Proverbs 13:24, 14:3, 13-14, and 23.

These verses may sound harsh but lovingly disciplining children so that they might learn, is far more loving than letting them have their way, and they be lost to foolishness and wickedness. Again hopefully your parents love you enough to discipline you but either way, there are other options (though not as beneficial).

The first option we will explore is to find a mentor. This should not only be someone that can teach you but they should also have standards. When you do not fulfill your end of the bargain they should be unwilling to budge. A good mentor will share their wisdom but ensure you learn the discipline necessary to use it.

As well, you are wise to call upon true friends to act as accountability partners. I recall in Jr. High when some friends, desiring to stop cursing, would have their accountability partners sock them in the arm any time they heard a foul word. Accountability partners are great but they are useless if there is never any downside to breaking the rules.

Finally, you should seek to discipline yourself. Do not lie and cheat yourself. Set rules and standards and deprive yourself of the reward if you fail to meet the minimum requirements of the task. For many years, I have been an excellent employee; working for hours in crappy jobs to give the best work possible. However, any time I approached my personal projects I was my own worst employee. I would watch some YouTube first or play a game. I stole time and potential from myself and I only became a speaker and author of this book by demanding more of myself. Notably, I set a schedule with myself, booking times and appointments that could not be missed or rescheduled. These appointments had specific goals to meet and not meeting them meant sacrificing leisure time to finish.

The above groups come in handy for self-discipline and personal goals because they help hold your feet to the fire when you are slacking, and they can pick you up in the downtimes. Once my wife saw I was serious about my intentions on this book she fully expected me to meet the goals. If we did something that caused me to miss a me-appointment to work on the book, the following day/days were rearranged so that the task was completed. It is important that you study your weaknesses and plan against them. Personally, I have a problem with YouTube and procrastination. A couple of methods I have I used to avoid these stumble blocks are to: 1) set time constraints (app enforced) on devices so that I can't binge-watch forever and 2) make appointments to incrementally work on projects and when other things come up making notes so I can stay on track.

To procrastinators, if you are like me, you have done some of your best work at the last minute; don't use that as justification. I can recall my only all-nighter in college required writing a paper for an 8 A.M. class. Jamming to the power of Twenty One Pilots' album *Blurryface* may have fueled me to create a paper that received an A, but I missed a night of sleep just because I was lazy and irresponsible. I have concluded we procrastinate because it forces us to prioritize the most immediate task. Ultimately our schedule is dictated by a vague priority hierarchy and external deadlines; we are left only focusing on that which is most important to complete at that given moment.

But there is no freedom in that! Your whole life is then dictated by the needs of others as you rush around trying to keep up. You can, however, break this mold by choosing to make each work session (appointment) important. I made this book an important task so every time I sat down I found it easy to pen my thoughts. Why? Because there were no other matters on my mind or to-do list for that time period.

Again, plan against your weaknesses. If you are always late adjust your schedule and make it necessary to be early. As an added motivation and value, being early will remove unneeded stress which we all could use. I also recently heard someone recommend the five-second challenge which I liked. If you are trying to make a choice, stop, count to five, and then immediately jump to action. This could be like talking to your crush or for the context of this paragraph getting out of bed so you are not late. Don't set alarms so you can snooze them; that will only train yourself to not wake up. Instead, when your alarm goes off, get up at that moment knowing you have been blessed with a new day of life. Don't waste the first hour of it rolling in bed and dragging your heels squandering the limited heartbeats we all have.

These are just some random examples but I hope you can see the benefit of identifying your weaknesses and being proactive to plan against them. One area that you should definitely practice self-discipline in is bad habits. The most obvious are time-sucking leeches like TV, YouTube, social media, games, etc. When you look back on your life are you really going to be glad that you spent multiple hours a day mindlessly seeking 5-second entertainment? Things like TikTok are popular because we have trained ourselves to only enjoy that which is immediately consumable. Instead, think of that time being well spent on a hobby, studying, or face-to-face conversations *gasp*.

The last thing I would like to speak on is "addictions". These can come in the forms of porn, alcohol, drugs, etc. Not to completely simplify these issues, but simply these areas are not problems because you are an addict but because you have a sin problem. Maybe you rely on them through feeling lonely, depressed, grief, guilt, or simply pleasure, any way you cut it these vices are just being used to fill a void.

The first step is to get help. If you have a chemical dependence on some substance find a program that will help you detox. But when that's done you have one more problem, yourself. You may not have a chemical pull to the substance but you still have the same mental struggles which will drag you back down. This is why it's necessary to address the sin; you must repent of your sins and trust in Christ. He is the one true cure to loneliness, depression, grief, and guilt; and, He leads you to things that are rightfully joyful and pleasurable. Fix the dependence if that is needed but don't forget to address your spiritual need for a savior.

On porn, adultery (premarital included aka fornication), and lust you must stop cold turkey. Place your needs fully on Christ and take every thought captive. The Bible says to cut off the hand and eye that sins against you. Don't physically harm yourself but put down, lock up, or sell the smartphone, laptop, TV, or magazines hindering you. It's a mental and spiritual war that you will never make progress in by lingering beside the tempter. Proverbs talks of not even going down the street of the harlot lest you be tempted and fall into ruin. Don't even go near that which causes problems and have accountability partners that hold you to it.

[Proverbs 5:1-14 NASB95] 1 My son, give attention to my wisdom, Incline your ear to my understanding; 2 That you may observe discretion And your lips may reserve knowledge. 3 For the lips of an adulteress drip honey And smoother than oil is her speech; 4 But in the end she is bitter as wormwood, Sharp as a two-edged sword. 5 Her feet go down to death, Her steps take hold of Sheol. 6 She does not

ponder the path of life; Her ways are unstable, she does not know it. 7 Now then, my sons, listen to me And do not depart from the words of my mouth. 8 Keep your way far from her And do not go near the door of her house, 9 Or you will give your vigor to others And your years to the cruel one; 10 And strangers will be filled with your strength And your hard-earned goods will go to the house of an alien; 11 And you groan at your final end, When your flesh and your body are consumed; 12 And you say, "How I have hated instruction! And my heart spurned reproof! 13 "I have not listened to the voice of my teachers, Nor inclined my ear to my instructors! 14 "I was almost in utter ruin In the midst of the assembly and congregation."

Taking every thought captive entails reigning in your mind to not go down rabbit trails of progressive wickedness and also actively changing your thoughts towards the stumbling block. Pastor Doug Wilson has an excellent YouTube video on Nuisance Lust which describes this; the practice is also good for a variety of mental warfare. A short example, a boy is walking through the mall and sees a good-looking gal with clothing that does not leave much to the imagination. His thoughts immediately jump to lusting after her. It is at this moment that he must immediately act! He should turn his eyes away, repent for his immediate sinful thought, and then replace it with a godly thought. Going from "man she is hot" to "Lord make her beautiful in Christ and free her from the world's distorted version of beauty."

Thinking this way is not an excuse to linger beside the temptation. Rather it is a method to process the thought rightly so that it may pass out of your mind. If you attempt to suppress and "manhandle" your sins you will only fall on your face time and time again. This is because we need to process thoughts and trying to unthink the thought will only keep the thought in your mind. The other reason is that we desperately need Christ to strengthen us for He alone has lived a sinless life though being tempted every way we could be. The "secret" I have found to this is seen in the Bible, I just had to be humble enough to implement it properly. Believers are promised that they will not encounter a temptation that they are not also given a way to escape or overcome. We are promised that we can overcome any temptation but to do so we must not try to manhandle it but rather humble ourselves to the strength Christ is giving us and overcome them. If we try to ignore this call to submit to God's way then we will keep relying on our own strength and continuously fall on our face.

The last area of criticism before a more positive note is staying healthy. All of these things I am bringing up, I am both speaking from love and as a lesson to myself. Unfortunately, I am not good about personal health and my "old man" body proves it. If you want to be a generally happier, more energetic person, eat right and workout. Eat good, healthy foods but also realize that controlling your portions goes a long way as well. I easily lost 10 pounds just by being intentional about what I was eating and how much. Another little helper is the "5 To 1 Rule". To follow this you must read the total carbs and the total fiber on the nutrition label. Once you get your numbers, divide the total carbs by the total fiber, and ideally, the result should be no greater than 5 carbs per 1 fiber. Watching your serving sizes/snacking and following the 5 To 1 Rule will go a long way.

And yes, expending energy makes energy. Regularly working out will boost the amount of energy your body makes. It also gives you more strength and stamina to live your normal life easier. Think about it, if you walk 5,000 steps a day your body will only be comfortable walking 5,000 steps; but if you workout every day your body will produce more energy to meet the demand and make those 5,000 steps easier to accomplish. Finally, don't discredit stretching. I am against yoga and there are plenty of alternative stretches you can do to help strengthen your body. The human body is intricately woven together in ways we only partially understand. I have a problem where a bad right ankle has caused my left shoulder to go bad, crazy right!? Stretching helps strengthen the bonds between muscle groups

> *Yoga is a religious practice with each position representing a false god. As well its view of meditation is unbiblical because it practices clearing the mind whereas the Bible says to meditate on God's word.*

as well as help muscles recuperate. This is why glute and thigh stretches helps mend lower back pain. If you have specific pains try discovering what muscles it might be and use stretches that target them. When I started grooming horses, I would walk around the horse barn almost literally dragging my leg but focused stretching helped relax and buildup those aching muscles over time.

All of the previous topics are greatly aided by the principle of always doing something hard. If I had stopped grooming horses because it was too hard physically, I never would have learned to stretch nor stuck around for the four months that it took for my body to be fully acclimated to the physical labor. I only became a lean mean grooming machine through disciplined stretching, constant repetition, and pushing through the hard work.

> Our stable was in Dallas from April to August and my horses were on the North side of the barn… which means there were plenty of 110-degree afternoons I had to clean stalls and fill hay bags with basically zero wind except for each horse's fan (which felt more like a heater blowing). Why would I go through that? Because I loved the job and I was there to work. So what if the temperatures were awful, there is so much accomplishment in doing a hard day's work especially when the going gets tough. The crappy jobs and situations should be embraced not shunned.

Actively pursue that which is challenging and hard. I like the quote from a retired Army Ranger, Major Jeff Strueker, *"Hard times don't last but hard men do….. Get up tomorrow and do something difficult and put yourself to the test."* An encouragement I heard preacher Paul Washer say about reading the Bible more is that 'those who have a great ability to read the Word are not more gifted in that area. It is just as hard for them as it is for you or me. Those individuals however make a point and plan to read the Word and that makes all the difference' [paraphrase]. Don't make excuses, discipline is what you need, not some talent, gift, or IQ score.

Here are some ideas:

- Take a cold shower.
  - Besides having some physical benefits it will teach you to be mentally strong when you are physically uncomfortable. (I suggest the Wim Hof Method but would encourage you to avoid the Yoga).
- Study something new or that you are weak in. Try memorizing Bible verses and catechisms so you have good solid truths to call upon in all situations.

You get the idea, there are things you know you should be doing so do them even though you don't want to.

"It never pays to be lazy." Memorize that and live by it. I created that phrase to tell to myself years ago; it is a lesson I learned the hard way oh so many times. This is similar to "if something is worth doing, it's worth doing it right". If you take the lazy path you will almost always create more work for yourself, cause a bigger mess, and do a poorer job. The simplest and most practical analogy I have is when you take out the trash and don't replace the bag. I can't tell you how many times I got angry at myself because I would take out the trash, put off rebagging the can, need to throw something away an hour later, and then be annoyed that I didn't have a bag in the can. That is something so incredibly mundane and simple but man it can be easy to listen to the voice of laziness and get so mad at yourself because of it.

Ultimately, be responsible and consistent and you will be so much happier with yourself. When you cheat yourself, you can only be mad at yourself. Take care of your responsibilities and do it when you can, said, and should. Dave Ramsey has two great quotes, "Live like no one else so later you can live like no one else." and "Being willing to delay pleasure for a greater result is a sign of maturity." Simply, live by delayed gratification. Do what you should do, not what you want to do. Doing what you should do will help create time for what you want to do; this will allow you to enjoy your free time more fully. Since I mentioned Dave Ramsey, I highly recommend going through Financial Peace University because self-discipline with money will make your life so much simpler and better.

I guess the obvious summary is practicing self-discipline will cause you to be a much happier and better person. Examine yourself and find ways to integrate two of the ideas I shared, immediately, in pursuit of greater self-discipline.

Chapter 3

Morality

Morality - Beliefs about what is right behavior and what is wrong behavior [Merriam-Webster]

We all operate with some level of morality and make decisions depending on the heading of our personal moral compasses. The interesting thing about morality though is we all generally operate off of the same morals whether you are a devout Christian, Buddhist, or Atheist. Obviously, there may be some exceptions such as serial killers or even remote tribes that practice cannibalism (or any manner of other things) but even in those circumstances, I believe the same morals still exist; they are just suppressed in an extreme manner of what we personally do when breaking our own moral codes.

An excellent example of this is the legend of how some Native Americans viewed the conscience as a triangle in the stomach. Anytime you did wrong the triangle would jab you (ever felt the sickening pain of guilt?) to signal a need to correct your wrongdoing. Along with that, there was a warning not to ignore the signal lest the points "jab" you so often that they be rounded off and it no longer pain you to do wrong. The Bible describes this as a continuous hardening of one's heart towards sin. I think it is telling that Native Americans did not have foreign contact (for only God knows how long) yet they had a system to describe conscience and morality.

For this, if we look to the Bible, which is far superior to all psychology books combined, in explaining the human condition, we see that we all have a conscience and it always starts with the same parameters because the law of God is written on each of our hearts. You need not look further than the 10 commandments to validate this. In reverse order:

10. Thou shalt not covet   *9. Thou shall not bear false witness*

8. Thou shall not steal   *7. Thou shall not commit adultery*

6. Thou shall not murder   *5. Honor the Father and Mother*

4. Remember the Sabbath   *3. Thou shall not take God's name in vain*

2. Thou shall not worship graven images   *1. Thou shall have no other gods before Me*

If we are being honest with ourselves we all agree to some level that the last six are wrong to break. Sure we make excuses for some of them but, for example, even though we will lie we don't appreciate being lied to. Number five we know we should obey however we often do not and we are all guilty of the first four commandments. We attempt to not validate the statements of one through four by hiding behind gods of other religions or the gods of our own creation (sports, atheism, significant others, etc.) but at the end of the day they are true and we are breaking them.

In the New Testament, Jesus summarizes the whole law of the Old Testament (which is much longer than the big ten) into two simple commandments.

37 And He [Jesus] said to him, " 'YOU SHALL LOVE THE LORD YOUR GOD WITH ALL YOUR HEART, AND WITH ALL YOUR SOUL, AND WITH ALL YOUR MIND.' 38 "This is the great and foremost commandment. 39 "The second is like it, 'YOU SHALL LOVE YOUR NEIGHBOR AS YOURSELF.' 40 "On these two commandments depend the whole Law and the Prophets." [Mat 22:37-40 NASB95]

If we should expect others to follow our rules when playing games, how much more should the thrice-holy God expect us to live by His laws which He wrote on our hearts and in His letter to us (the Bible)? Here we have Christ summarizing the law in that God is looking for us to fully love Him first of all and to love our neighbors as ourselves. If we operate from that lens we can abide by our internal compass. (Though our sinful flesh wages war to drag us into all manner of lawlessness.)

Again, I must say that abiding by these laws are impossible and, even if they were not, you have already failed in at least one point and are therefore guilty of breaking all the law. The knowledge I share in this book is no more profitable to you than a match is to a book lest you surrender to the Lordship of Christ, His all-sufficient work on the cross, and His resurrection from the dead. To that point, the match is not only unprofitable, it also carries great ability to de-

stroy the book; likewise is this knowledge to you (I of-
fer no returns for anyone that tests that hypothesis on
this book **:)**)

> [Jas 2:10-11 NASB95] 10 For whoever keeps the whole law
> and yet stumbles in one [point,] he has become guilty of all.
> 11 For He who said, "DO NOT COMMIT ADULTERY,"
> also said, "DO NOT COMMIT MURDER." Now if you
> do not commit adultery, but do commit murder, you have
> become a transgressor of the law.

That said, I would like to think practically about
the greatest two commandments at this time. If we
love the Lord our God, Creator, and Father then we
should obey His commandments. We should cease
doing that which He hates and start doing that which
He loves. Todd Freil, host of Wretched Radio, used an
example of two friends and apples that I will liberally
paraphrase.

*You and I are friends and being friends I know that
you hate the taste, smell, and appearance of apples [and I'll
even throw in you're allergic to them]. However, knowing
all of this [and being mindful of it] when I come over to
your house one day I intentionally come in the door munch-
ing on a big ole Honeycrisp. All in a moment you are en-
raged, sick to your stomach, and starting to wheeze.*

*Now would that be very loving to you? Would you
say that I'm best friend material for doing something like
that? No! It is hateful, cruel, and vile to act in such a manner to your friend!*

*Then why do we do that to God when he has written
down all the things He hates?*

Do we hate the things God hates? Do we repent
and turn from our wrongdoings to the things which

He has called us to do? We will never be perfect in this life but do we desire to serve God and love Him with all our heart, soul, and mind?

Seek to be a servant of others, whether you be a janitor or the president, have a servant's heart. This is demonstrated in concerning others before yourself whether it be outward, like only eating after everyone is served, or inward by leading your family or team in decisions that were made for their best interest. In both of these cases, you must concern yourself as an afterthought. Don't use these examples to elevate yourself; such as eating last to pile servings 1,2, and 3 on your plate (though that is clever) or telling your family that moving will be good for everyone when the only person that gains is your rung on the corporate ladder. If we are in a place of authority, whether in a business or at home, we need to use that authority but wisely. Be confident and make resolute decisions on behalf of those under you but again it should be decisions for the best of others. Using your position for your own good is selfish and prideful.

A Contentious But Useful Analogy

I am going to give a demonstration on how we can thoughtfully operate with a "love your neighbor as yourself" mindset but the subject matter is difficult because there are two distinct camps arguing on this issue. I heard a Christian politician immediately make this application and I will share it with you now.

The issue in question is whether or not we should build a wall on our southern border. Plenty say "YES!" and plenty say "NO!" but instead of getting into common talking points let us just ask "what would be loving to our neighbors?" When discussing Mexico it does not take very long for the cartels to come up. These cartels predominantly control Mexico and hold influence over government officials, law enforcement, and the community by means of bribery and/or threats. This is not a universal rule but it is not uncommon for young people to be pressured into being in and aiding gangs; to be outside of them leaves you in a dangerous "gray" area.

These gangs and cartels have built their wealth and power off of the American people primarily through drug smuggling. Daily Mexicans, living and dead (they will often store drug shipments and contraband in dead bodies), come across the border illegally at the control of these cartels to grow their drug business. Often times these men, women, and children simply want to come to America for a better life but after paying the cartel to get them across they become essentially indentured servants (almost slaves) doing the bidding of the cartels. If they are lucky they may pay off their debt but likely the cartels will keep control over them even in America (whether by threatening their life or the lives of family and friends still in Mexico).

My question to you is "should we let this continue to happen?" I would hope that your answer is no, so then what can we do to stop it? Well the New York Times reported in October of 2021 that in the previous 12 months 1.7 million illegal immigrants were encountered. 1.7 million are just the ones encountered... Not all of those are Mexicans, plenty were just trying to seek refuge in the good ole USA (but also these cartels are not purely of Mexican decent). Furthermore, LawEnforcementToday.com reported in June of 2021 that roughly the daily average of "got-a ways" is 1,600! And these are just the ones they observed/encountered. Just imagine if we had a strong physical and technologically advanced border that got that number down to 10 a day. That would be a 160 times reduction (and I believe our border patrol could do/wants to do far better than that if they were adequately supported).

So making the illegal activity at the border change from a raging river to a tiny leak could drastically affect the way of life for Mexicans (and other countries that rely on our illegal activities) and the way of life for Americans. If the cartels could no longer get their product to the American people then overtime they would have to turn their efforts elsewhere. But considering America has the largest import of these drugs (considering other nations are further away, have their own sources, or can create it locally) the cartel's power and wealth would drastically decrease. This would allow the wonderful people (and I truly mean that. I legitimately love working with Mexicans and other Hispanic people) of Mexico to finally begin building a prosperous nation that I'm positive they want. Trust me; the Mexican culture has deep family and community roots; that is why so often only one family representative comes to America for work so that they can send the money back to the others. Mexico needs the opportunity to flourish and it's a legit question on whether or not the border could help advance that process.

If we could build a wall and a process that could significantly hinder illegal activity, aid in the capture of criminals, and ease the process for well-meaning immigrants this could only benefit both America and Mexico! Mexico could develop as a nation, finally being freed from the cartel's power; as a bonus American's safety and health would also increase. It's a common idea that drug dealers aren't in business to sell drugs they are in business to make addicts because any good businessman will tell you that return customers are the best customers. With decreased access to hard drugs, the health of many Americans would improve; not to mention the DEA (Drug Enforcement Administration) could focus more efforts locally to catch dealers instead of focusing on the sources abroad. But further securing our southern border would greatly hinder the horrid crimes of human and sex trafficking. Many Americans are kidnapped and smuggled from their families every year to enter slavery as laborers or more often to be raped by disgusting, perverted clientele.

If a border wall is able to even slightly decrease drug, human, sex, and contraband trafficking we owe that to our American and Mexican neighbors. To build the wall would be a loving olive branch to begin the process. To universally open up the border to anyone is unloving because the illegal activity would only increase, costing the lives of many innocent people. And this goes back to the idea of

Not to mention many jobs will be threatened by illegal immigrants willing to work for less with no tax obligation. The Biden administration's lax policies on the border (lax actually is probably more strict than reality) has even made illegals "super citizens" with greater rights than all actual citizens.

discipline. It is unloving to not punish children so that they can be delivered from their wrongdoing and therefore become a better person. Likewise, not punishing illegal immigrants will give them the freedom to continue breaking laws and abusing America; instead of desiring to benefit the country and community.

I hope through even this controversial topic you can see how putting politics aside we can just consider the second greatest commandment on how to view this issue. The following are just a further set of random examples to help you begin thinking on how to apply theses morality concepts. I must once again state that moral perfectionism is a doctrine that will send you straight to Hell. Salvation is only found in the finished work of Christ on the cross and His resurrection from the grave. Once we have accepted Christ as our savior we should begin to implement these concepts and even more biblical concepts into our lives so that, in the power of the Holy Spirit, seek to glorify God in all things and fulfill the greatest commandment.

Brief Points of Example (aka many mini-rants)

Since I have already brought up a taboo subject I will add this one last thing... I think. Hiring / promoting / selecting a person for a job / position / scholarship / etc. based on their skin color or sex is incredibly racists and /or sexist.

How can this be?! Well, let us imagine you worked a long 40 year career as a blue Martian in a red Martian society. Over those 40 years you did a good, honest job and earned the respect and friendship of all your red Martian neighbors and coworkers. Eventually there comes a day when a new position opens up that you and a few other red Martians are uniquely qualified for given your expertise and experience. Yet even though there is this handful of qualified individuals out of the clear green (well I can't use blue can I because that would be colorist...) an unqualified blue Martian that just came into town gets the job.

What?! How could they do this to you and the others! They say it's to show diversity and inclusion of the blues into the red's society; but what does that have to do with getting the job done?! This is just a case of identity politics trying to pander to another group. Instead of advancing the blues, in one fell swoop they have discredited all you have done to show the reds what you blues can do!

This thinking is all too common today in the incredibly racist and sexist ideologies of CRT (Critical Race Theory) and DEI (Diversity, Equity, and Inclusion).

Again, regard others more highly than yourself. This can be applied in all aspects of life. Two that come to mind are do not litter; first it is against the law (and also God's law) but also some person has to pick that trash up because you were too lazy to find a trash can. (Well not you specifically because I am sure anybody reading this book is far

Some places don't add bags but I know a city park that has trash bin holders with no trash bins and people constantly though garbage into the holder not paying attention to the fact it is just passing through to the ground, And again someone has to pick it up.

too courteous to purposefully litter). When throwing away trash, make sure to check that the container is bagged. Similarly, if/when you're driving remember that you are operating a 2,000 pound projectile that can easily crash vehicles, destroy surrounding land/buildings, and kill others as well as yourself. Pay attention! Being glued to your phone, lost in thought/music, or reckless driving endangers your-self and others. Beyond that, also follow the laws for your own good while also remembering to consider others first. I can't tell you how many people I have seen run a red light (which kills plenty of victims each year) because they thought themselves and their commute was more important than others and the law. As a bonus enter freeways at freeway speeds as a courtesy to those on it and again it's also for your safe-ty. Don't force everyone to play (or drive) at your lev-el just because you are too lazy to put in any effort. Obviously you can still be courteous when others don't press the gas to merge with you as well.

Love others as yourself. This doesn't mean to hate yourself or that you are of no value and signifi-cance but rather that a life lived to the love of God is aided by our humility of self for the gain of others.

In 2nd Peter, we are called to moral excellence/virtue. Let us be people that are known for taking the high road. Let us be people that are glorifying God in eve-rything that we do and especially in how we treat oth-ers. We shouldn't be doing this as a point of "virtue signaling" but rather just having such a deep concern of the things of God and those made in His image that those around us can't help but notice.

[Phl 2:1-7 NASB95] 1 *Therefore if there is any encour-agement in Christ, if there is any consolation of love, if there is any fellowship of the Spirit, if any affection and compassion, 2 make my joy complete by being of the same mind, maintaining the same love, united in spirit, intent on one purpose. 3 Do nothing from selfishness or empty conceit, but with humility of mind regard one another as more important than yourselves; 4 do not [merely] look out for your own personal interests, but also for the interests of others. 5 Have this attitude in yourselves which was also in Christ Jesus, 6 who, alt-hough He existed in the form of God, did not regard equality with God a thing to be grasped, 7 but emptied Himself, taking the form of a bond-servant, [and] being made in the likeness of men.*

Chapter 4

Contentment

[Phl 4:11-13 NASB95]11 Not that I speak from want, for I have learned to be content in whatever circumstances I am. 12 I know how to get along with humble means, and I also know how to live in prosperity; in any and every circumstance I have learned the secret of being filled and going hungry, both of having abundance and suffering need. 13 I can do all things through Him who strengthens me.

We fickle humans are always overly concerned about that which we can't control. This, impart, leads us into varied bouts of anxiety. "What's God's will for my life?!" "Where am I going for school?" "Should I take a gap year?" "What job do I want to pursue?" "Who should I marry?" "Furthermore, how am I going to make this happen and how can I pay for it!?!?". If you are over the age of 16 these questions have likely bounced through your head and many more.

Most people know the verse Phil 4:13 (seen above) but it is almost always separated from its preceding verses which give the verse its true power. Paul talks about having reached the pinnacle of contentment and being able to delight in and glorify God in any scenario, hungry or full. Through that, he has learned the truth of Phil 4:13; that he can rest in the strength of Christ and His provision to overcome all circumstances.

[Rom 8:28 NASB95] 28 And we know that God causes all things to work together for good to those who love God, to those who are called according to [His] purpose.

Why do we worry and fear when our creator is our provider? Learn to be content in all things for He is working all things together for your good, if you are one who loves Him. How does this apply to the above questions? Well, are you willing to stay in your present situation while you work towards something better? If you are in school are you willing to be content/patient with your situation until you can move on to the next step in life? Further, are you maximizing your time at your present stage in life so that when the next stage comes up you are ready for it? Or are you like my father who learned to be content in being a teacher to raise a family instead of chasing riches. There are times in life when we should have contentment knowing that we sacrificed self for the important things such as family.

I don't want to send you into a panic attack; these are not issues resolved in a day but they need to be on the chopping block sooner rather than later. OG motivational speaker Les Brown shares this idea very well in a story about him becoming a disc jockey, aka radio DJ (look up the YouTube clip its powerful and hilarious). A key idea he shares is that his mentor challenged him to practice being a DJ so that he would be ready when the opportunity arose. The elusive "door" that you are eagerly waiting to find open will likely one day present itself. When that day comes will you be able to barge through and make the most of the opportunity or will you squander your one chance? Les, in his story, eventually gets an opportunity to hit the airwaves and his practice caused his boss to be grateful instead of furious. Will you be prepared as well when opportunity comes a knockin'?

The biggest opponent to contentment is entitlement. You cannot have peace in your situation if you are constantly seeking what you're "owed". Before I get any further I will say it is okay to consider seeking a raise, promotion or new job; but you shouldn't ex-pect to get your way. Instead as time goes by (considering your goals, needs, and value added) you should seek advancement while being content to remain as you are; because as pastor Voddie Baucham would say, we are always "doing better than we deserve ".

Entitlement ruins contentment because it feeds off of pride and selfishness; telling yourself that "you deserve a raise and pat on the back" (often, you have only "earned" it in your own mind). You have a right to try and abound (Paul certainly did at times) and ask for a raise/promotion but your boss also has the freedom to say "yes" or "no" as they please. If they say yes, you ought to work hard to validate their decision; if they say no, that is okay and you should continue to be the best employee possible. In all this, again, you should not be operating from an entitled attitude that says pridefully, "I earned this!" nor "I'll show them they were wrong!" I used the job example but entitlement can rear its ugly head with your parents, at school, among peers, on the road, etc.

This is your life, take ownership of it and don't demand others come at your beck and call. Your parents aren't required to wait on your every desire; if you want a car, video game, or fun money, get up and find a means to provide it for yourself. Your significant other or your friends don't exist to make you happy and you should be considerate of their wants and needs and interests. In school, your teachers are there to teach you, not to supply endless extra-credit because you chose to blow off a test (as if it is a crime that they give you a failing grade. Psh yeah-right, you certainly earned any "F's"). Lastly, the government exists to provide law, order, and infrastructure to a country, not to endlessly support people too lazy to provide for themselves.

While not in all cases, welfare promotes laziness and poverty. In the words of the excellent economist Thomas Sowell *"You cannot take any people, of any color, and exempt them from the requirements of civilization -- including work, behavioral standards, personal responsibility and all the other basic things that the clever intelligentsia disdain -- without ruinous consequences to them and to society at large."*[2] And as well the Bible says *[2Th 3:10 NASB95] 10 For even when we were with you, we used to give you this order: if anyone is not willing to work, then he is not to eat, either.*

---

[2] Sowell, Thomas. "Blame the Welfare State, Not Racism, for Poor Blacks' Problems: Thomas Sowell." Pennlive, Penn Live, 7 May 2015, https://www.pennlive.com/opinion/2015/05/poor_blacks_looking_for_someo n.html.

We don't deserve anything in this life except for God's judgment for breaking His law (if we are still reading this then He has graciously permitted us continued life). To expect the world to revolve around us is foolish when we really should be thankful for every last breath. We live in the most spectacular age in human history (at least as far as technology is concerned) and truly we all have the perfect setup to succeed in life. We all have our unique situations but that is just fuel for who you can be. Remember, there is a creator who is sovereign over all things, even our "crappy" situation. Our situation and life is God ordained so don't shout "woe is me" but rejoice in who you get to be!

> [Pro 16:9 NASB95]
> 9 The mind of man plans his way, But the LORD directs his steps.

We are always doing better than we deserve because there is inevitably somebody doing worse than us and again God should have struck us down already as it is; so don't throw a "pity party" but a "potential party"! Learn to leverage your situation to develop and grow. Consider this starter pack of resources that you already have access to:

- <u>What do you know?</u>
  - Just because you might be in a new situation doesn't mean you can't utilize prior knowledge and experience.
- <u>Who do you know?</u>
  - You'd be surprised how true the "7 Degrees of Kevin Bacon" can be at times.
- <u>What Resources Are Available?</u>
  - The Local Library

- Internet
- Computers
- Research
- And....BOOKS
- Your Community
  - Local Clubs/Interests
  - Local Wants/Needs (Great for the entrepreneurs out there)
  - Businesses
  - Free/Paid Programs and Coaching
  - Schools

With all of my innovations, I would have gotten nowhere without my dad's shop, my engineering teacher, expert friends (drum players, horse trainers, etc.), my family lineage of tinkering, my youth pastor, my job that provided the funds, the Lord that put it all together, etc. You were divinely placed in your situation/location, at this time, as your unique person to affect the world in only the way you can. I appreciate the sentiment I see/hear occasionally "no one can help everyone but everyone can help someone". Whether you are Elon Musk or you work in a cubicle, only you have your sphere of influence and your life. Don't envy others when you have what they don't, yourself.

Whereas entitlement is a great enemy to contentment, patience is a great friend. Impatience is a very troublesome characteristic (as seen in my intro) that often leads to a lack of development and productivity. This happens because we get so caught up chasing the future that we don't capitalize on the present. This is applicable to our jobs, schooling, personal life, mental health and more. Always needing that thing down the road causes a lack of contentment but also leaves us undeveloped for the future. Leverage your here and now and when opportunity comes knocking you will be ready to step into that next chapter. Have patience my young padawan for you have plenty of years left, Lord willing, to accomplish more than you can imagine.

Guarding Yourself Against Discontentment

There is also a societal cancer that is causing much discontentment and grief. If you desire to be content you will need to guard yourself against this enemy. It touts itself as a helpful system to right all of society's problems but in the process destroys society further. The primary issue is that the system is built off of identity politics and gives every identity a rating. As it so happens, because I am a straight white male that identifies as a conservative and also a Christian my societal standing is rock bottom (let it be said if that did put me at the top I'd still hate the system). On the other hand the top of the hierarchy are transgender minority immigrants that are liberal atheists (secret bonus points if you are a pedophile). Every person gets a rating and that dictates if you will be hired, accepted into university, whether or not you can comment on an issue, and more. The system is supposedly designed to fight racism but it is in fact radically racist inside and out!

Such a system tells black children that they are destined to be uneducated and oppressed by the villainous white man; for these reasons they must vote for liberal politicians to be their defenders and providers (a.k.a. a clever way to guarantee votes). It also

undermines the effort of those who have built up rep-
utations and made something of themselves. Imagine
you are a black Christian female applying for a $200k
per year job at the company you have worked at for 20
years. You have the experience, knowledge, degree,
etc. but your company being "woke" hires an applicant with no experience and an unrelated degree
simply because that applicant is a black transgender
female (bio male). Their desire to have a workplace of
"Diversity, Equity, and Inclusion" gave them the
"right" to spit in your face and say "we don't care
about you or your reputation".

While this may have been somewhat of a tan-
gent, the above system represents the aforementioned
DEI (Diversity, Equity, and Inclusion) and CRT (Critical Race Theory) which robs humans of contentment
because we should be celebrating our differences, not
starting wars. America has always been a melting pot
of people and any trip to the grocery store is a wonderful match-up of Americans in all shapes, sizes, and
shades.

Yes there are plenty of other issues leading to
discontentment and I'll be honest this country is far
beyond being in a pickle. God annihilated Sodom and
Gomorrah for their sins and we, having been founded
as a Christian nation, are due for much greater wrath
and judgment. It is long been time to repent and turn
back to Christ if America is to exist much longer.
Learn to see others as humans, neighbors, friends, and
family. When going through that mixed bag of people
at the grocery store don't look to judge and categorize
them with some sense of superiority (after all your
there with them). But think on this, we all have our

different backgrounds, stories, and issues but all of us are Americans. Further we are all descendants of Adam and share the same blood. Lastly, if saved:

[Rom 10:12 NASB95] 12 ...there is no distinction between Jew and Greek; for the same [Lord] is Lord of all, abounding in riches for all who call on Him;

Be grateful, patient, and content in the present so that as time goes on you, like the Apostle Paul, can learn "... the secret of being filled and going hungry, both of having abundance and suffering need." Contentment is a beautiful thing. This chapter laid out some principles to achieve it but the last contributors are those things that bring about Fulfillment.

[Mat 6:25-34 NASB95] 25 "For this reason I say to you, do not be worried about your life, [as to] what you will eat or what you will drink; nor for your body, [as to] what you will put on. Is not life more than food, and the body more than clothing? 26 "Look at the birds of the air, that they do not sow, nor reap nor gather into barns, and [yet] your heavenly Father feeds them. Are you not worth much more than they? 27 "And who of you by being worried can add a [single] hour to his life? 28 "And why are you worried about clothing? Observe how the lilies of the field grow; they do not toil nor do they spin, 29 yet I say to you that not even Solomon in all his glory clothed himself like one of these. 30 "But if God so clothes the grass of the field, which is [alive] today and tomorrow is thrown into the furnace, [will He] not much more [clothe] you? You of little faith! 31 "Do not worry then, saying, 'What will we eat?' or 'What will we drink?' or 'What will we wear for clothing?' 32 "For the Gentiles eagerly seek all these things; for your heavenly Father knows that you need all these things. 33 "But seek first His kingdom and His righteousness, and all these things will be added to you. 34 "So do not worry about tomorrow; for tomorrow will care for itself. Each day has enough trouble of its own.

Chapter 5

Fulfillment

Raise your hand if you want to be on your death bed and say "Wow! What a waste of time that was"... This is a book so I am just going to assume/hope nobody raised their hand. Contentment and fulfillment are the biggest "tangibles" that we humans are after; they are best seen when flowing out of joy and purpose. In this final code, I would like to share some applications that promote fulfillment so you can examine your life and make a plan to discover ever-increasing fulfillment. Fulfillment comes last because you must be content to experience it.

Most people will either seek this attribute by asking "what do I want to do/be?" or "what is God's plan for my life?" and these questions can be daunting. I should know considering I went to school for Computer Science after years of desiring to be an architect, then I changed to Communications after a semester because I wanted to be speaker, then dropped out entirely to be an actor; all that and much more as I expressed earlier. Trust me I have warred with finding contentment and fulfillment for some time. I may not have fully arrived (and I am not sure we ever will in this life) but I will share what I have found beneficial throughout this chapter.

The most obvious start is what job should you have. By using the last four codes you should have a rough framework of who you are; so take your interests, abilities, and options to decide where to go. Don't focus on finding your "passion". Sure there may be something obvious but, most of all, your goal should be to find work that fits you and is enjoyable. I don't really like staring at a screen all day but I enjoy drafting and the compensation is what I need (focus on needs not your often vague worldly wants). So not surprisingly it is quite enjoyable to go to work. Nor does working seven days a week in manual labor for low pay sound like fun but the equine bug and working outside more than made up for it. In both cases I had a skill I was using, an aspect I found interesting, a job that was challenging, and could still meet my present needs.

What can you do, what do you like, what do you need and similar questions can help you decide what path to take. Along the way try to enjoy work for Work's sake. We were made and designed to work, learn to appreciate that feeling of accomplishment that you labored well and were as productive as possible.

26 Then God said, "Let Us make man in Our image, according to Our likeness; and let them rule over the fish of the sea and over the birds of the sky and over the cattle and over all the earth, and over every creeping thing that creeps on the earth." 27 God cre-

ated man in His own image, in the image of God He created him; male and female He created them. 28 God blessed them; and God said to them, "Be fruitful and multiply, and fill the earth, and subdue it; and rule over the fish of the sea and over the birds of the sky and over every living thing that moves on the earth." 29 Then God said, "Behold, I have given you every plant yielding seed that is on the surface of all the earth, and every tree which has fruit yielding seed; it shall be food for you; 30 and to every beast of the earth and to every bird of the sky and to every thing that moves on the earth which has life, [I have given] every green plant for food"; and it was so. 31 God saw all that He had made, and behold, it was very good. And there was evening and there was morning, the sixth day. [Gen 1:26-31 NASB95]

It also helps to practice the morality chapter and lean into outlets that promote selflessness. One of these is parenting. It is foolish to put your career before having children. It may not be for everyone (though I'd say they are outliers considering it is a command since the Garden of Eden) but, after you have settled into married life, don't put off parenting for long because it gives you an outlet to care for someone else. Parenting should only come about through marriage because it is how it was intended; God instituted marriage and then immediately parenting. As such, the roles of mother & father, female & male, are vitally important to your child's success. Children need a godly father and godly mother to raise them up in the nurture and admonition of the Lord (Ephesians 6:4 KJV). We are all going to screw it up to some degree but that is why it is so necessary to take it seriously and heed the biblical mandates and principles. God gave humanity the command to be fruitful and multiply; so the most God honoring thing we can do is to raise up children unto the Lord.

That leads to the next outlet, marriage. Marriage is a tremendous blessing that teaches you to communicate, love/respect another person, become one with another, and re-prioritize life from self and advancement to simply being happy if you get another day with your boo. I have heard it said (and can verify) marriage is a sanctifying experience; it's greatest blessings flow out when it is knit with biblical patterns and principles. In marriage two become one flesh and an undefiled marriage bed greatly aids in unity with your spouse. We must guard our hearts for we commit adultery (even outside of marriage) by lusting after others who are not our spouse (even when we haven't met them yet).

I need to also clarify that God created marriage and shared it in the Bible and, therefore, marriage is by definitional between one man and one woman. Any distortion of this, from an "open relationship "to sodomy (LGBT and such) robs you of any potential fulfillment because you're attacking God's natural working of creation. Such statements might make me a bigot but I am certain no fulfillment or any other blessing will be found there, as it (amongst other things) is an abomination to the Lord Any relationships that breaks God's intentions may look decent or admirable but it is certainly stemming from a love of evil and is corrupted fully.

This may sound obvious but you should not have a job, raise children, or get married just to leverage those people for fulfillment. These issues and others can bring about fulfillment when they are rooted by a motivation to honor and glorify God through following His word.

I will now share what should be our utmost priority, even before marriage (second priority) and parenting (third priority). This outlet and priority is to live for God. Our purpose in life is to glorify and honor God so it is natural that we can most find fulfillment there. A traditional Christian phrase is Soli Dio Gloria or "to God alone be the glory". The beauty of this statement is that it applies to every aspect of life. We should honor God in every thought, word, and deed. We should love our spouse and seek their needs but great unity is found in prioritizing Christ likeness who is the tuning fork that makes us harmonize. Parenting is a unique endeavor but this is squandered if we don't use that time to instruct them in the ways of the Lord. Hard work is great but pride, appeasing your boss, or just earning a paycheck are shallow motives; rather we could be working unto the Lord no matter our particular career or work situation.

Soli Dio Gloria is the pinnacle of why we exist. To deny it will only cause and promote evil motives and outcomes whereas abiding by it opens us up to delighting in our Creator and thus filling us with purpose and joy and fulfillment.

Conclusion

That's A Wrap

You finished it! I appreciate you surviving my many soapboxes and tangents. I firmly believe that the Codes of Self Innovation are just what the doctor ordered to get you on your feet and moving towards a fulfilling life. I hope that you now see how these codes fit into your life and desire to satisfy the requirements of each one.

I must once again state, however, that this book is nothing more than expensive kindling depending on what you do with Jesus Christ. I could site verses, Judeo-Christian history, secular and scientific supports, and more but at the end of the day, it's all just fluff. Ultimately, you either believe you are a helpless lawbreaker in need of salvation by the perfect God-Man of Jesus Christ who lived a perfect life, died on the cross, was buried, and rose bodily from the grave fully atoning for the sins of the world, or you do not believe that. Jesus said He was the way, the truth, the life, and the only way to the Father. Either He is a liar, lunatic, or Lord; which will you believe?

The tagline Have A Great Life (or HAGL) developed in high school because as an awkward introvert I never knew how to say goodbye. So somehow I started saying "Have a great life" when parting ways with my friends as a way to say goodbye; but also just in case we never met again, my hope would be that they have a great life. The shocking finality of the statement was always so stout that it signaled a fitting conclusion to our time together. So now that we have spent this time together I must conclude and you must depart back into the real world. Till we meet again either in text, audio, video, or face-to-face.

Thank you for your time; I trust this will have a profound impact on you as these lessons have done for me. May the grace of the Lord be upon you.

Have A Great Life,
Casey Williams

HAGL With Casey

Per my awkward salutation and my desire to be a motivational speaker, the business name of *HAGL With Casey* seemed fitting. The best way to reach me is via my website aptly named *haglwithcasey.com* where you will find info on me, my blog, and links to active social media pages.

If you, or someone you know, would like me to present The Codes of Self Innovation at your event please don't hesitate to reach out. I would be thrilled and honored to deliver these important topics to your audience.

One of the things I like to do is recommend resources that have helped me and may be beneficial to you. This is not an exhaustive list but contains sources that have helped me or that I hope can help you (if applicable)

Searching For A Church Home

I travelled a lot with the horses and had to practice finding a good church. Thankfully with these following sites and much prayer I arrived at good places every time. Personally, I believe the Reformed tradition is the best approach to the Bible and certainly if you are a new Christian, attending a Reformed church will rapidly progress your theology. Be sure to also read each church's Statement of Faith (which in good churches will be easily found on their website) and listen to a few of the recent sermons. Your discernment will strengthen overtime but in general avoid a church if the preaching sounds like a motivational speech, always lacks the Gospel, misuses or forgets the Bible, is all about you and not about God, and if it is heretical.

- *Founders.org/church-search/*
  - This is my primary resource
- *SermonAudio.com* or their app Sermon Audio
  - Not every good church is on SA but it helps to find sermons as well as having a Church Finder
- *9marks.org/church-search/*

Finally these sites can help. I will typically see what churches nearby populate on 2 out of the 3 sites and start researching from there. Through much care and prayer I trust the Lord will bring you to where you need to be. Once there get plugged in and don't jump ship at the drop of a hat, leaving a church should only be done out of necessity, not out of preference.

Finding Help With Bible Questions and Bible Study

You will find your favorite teacher and ministries overtime but here are some great resources to start your journey. These are listed in no particular

order and assume that you are in fact attend-
ing/seeking a local church and discussing with the
church elders as often as possible.

- Canon Press & Doug Wilson
  - *Canonpress.com* or their app Canon+ or
    YouTube.com/Canonpress or the blog at
    Dougwils.com are all ways to access their
    content. From books to shows to sermons
    to short topical videos Doug Wislon and
    Canonpress have helpful content for
    learning. Doug Wilson can be controver-
    sial but his views are well thought out
    and not heretical.
- Ligonier Ministries & R.C. Sproul
  - *Ligonier.org* or *Renewingyourmind.org* has
    various podcasts, radio programs,
    YouTube videos, video series, books, blog
    posts and more. I personally love using
    their resources when I need clarity on a
    specific Bible verse as you can filter by
    Scripture Index. Though R.C. Sproul has
    gone to be with the Lord his ministry con-
    tinues to provide great content.
- Truth For Life & Alistair Begg
  - Begg is a Scottish American pastor that
    has a unique gift of using illustrations,
    stories, and quotes to bring the text and
    application to life. He is a great preacher
    for everyone from laymen to scholars and
    is easy to listen to. They also have a
    YouTube channel, website, and app.
- One Passion Ministries & Steve Lawson

- o Steve Lawon is a true expositor that can make the most complex doctrines under-standable. He is most easily found on YouTube with sermons uploaded by var-ious channels. The One Passion Minsitries YouTube channel is famously home to *The Bible Study with Steve Lawson* which has been profitable to Christians the world over, myself included.
- Honorable Mentions
  - o Apologia studios
    - Esp helpful for Mormons, Jeho-vah's Witnesses, and Atheists
  - o Wretched Radio with Todd Friel
  - o Grace To You with John MacArthur
  - o Voddie Baucham
  - o Paul Washer
  - o Living Waters with Ray Comfort
  - o Truth Unites with Gavin Ortlund
    - Esp helpful for any Catholics and Orthodox
  - o Justin Peters
  - o Desiring God with John Piper
    - Ask Pastor John has short respons-es to many common questions
  - o The American Gospel Movies

The Mike Rowe S.W.E.A.T. Pledge

The single best secular summation of various points I have attempted to make in this book (esp. in regards to work) is the S.W.E.A.T. Pledge by the mikeroweWORKS Foundation. Learn the 12 pledges and live by them; your work ethic will thank you.

As a bonus, if you are considering going into the trades (which you should consider as equally as, or more so, College) the mikeroweWORKS Foundation gives Work Ethic Scholarships to help people like you so you can learn a trade and keep society running. https://www.mikeroweworks.org/sweat/

To Those Dealing With Homosexuality

To start I would encourage you to watch the film *In His Image: Delighting In God's Pan for Gender and Sexuality* on YouTube or their website *Inhisimage.movie* where they also have links to ministries that would love to talk with you and help you (Inhisimage.com/resources/ministries). Many of the above bring up the topic on occasion as well which can be helpful. I find content by Canonpress and Voddie Baucham to be excellent at challenging the doctrines of the world on this topic.

Escaping Addiction and Lust

Apologia Studies has produced some content on avoiding Alcoholics Anonymous and how to properly escape chemical dependence both physically and mentally.

Many of the above resources have content on pornography but I would specifically plead with you to view the Set Free Course at *SetFreeCourse.com* and/or the book *Passions of the Heart* by John D. Street. Yes you'll have to spend some money ($50 max for both) but it is vitally important that you be set free from pornography.

Finally I would also recommend both men and women to view Doug Wilson's *Dear Dawson* and *Dear Darla* series on YouTube to get a right view to your gender, the other gender, as well as sex and marriage. Paul Washer also has some sermon series geared to men and also marriage.